Power to Talk

Master the Art of Communication -
How to Build Better Relationship with Anyone

Rick Markley

Table of Contents

Introduction

The next time you're in a meeting or listening to someone and you're thinking to yourself, "Should I speak up here? Maybe it will be more trouble than its worth," I suggest to you that that's probably a good time to assert yourself.

Yes, occasionally you will go overboard and say too much. There will also be times when in retrospect it would have been better if you had said nothing. This will happen. This is life. Heed your internal voice.

If you think you ought to say something, the chances are extremely favorable. This is an instance in which it makes sense for you to speak up. You'll learn from those encounters and get better at training yourself to know when it's time to speak up.

This book will teach you how to build confidence to deal with anyone; whether it's family, friends, or co-workers. We all know that having good communication skills can be the difference between success and mediocrity.

1. Effective Speaking

Do you realize that for every half hour you speak to someone; you're producing a text equivalent of 20 transcribed pages? If you were to take such transcription, clean it up, and eliminate the redundancies, you'd end up with about 14 to 16 pages of material.

In other words, every 2 minute you're speaking to someone, you are creating a text equivalent to one manuscript page. So, there can be no more discussion about a lack of opportunity to get in some practice.

To understand who has vocal self-confidence, you need to pay attention to people that talk to you. Let's start with those who apparently do not have it. These are people who:

- Don't speak in clear, resonant tones.

- Stumble over their words.

- Use sentences punctuated by "um," "er," and "ah."

- Inject "you know," "it's like," and other verbal asides that only distract from a listener's ability to gain meaning.

Effective speaking increasingly is becoming a highly demanded attribute of rising career professionals. Nearly every organization wants technologically competent professionals that can reasonably articulate their thoughts.

I'm not saying you have to become an orator of the same caliber as William Jennings Bryan, develop the elocution skills of Winston Churchill, or make deliveries of the drama and emotion of Jesse Jackson; far from it. Indeed, some of the most persuasive people you may know, those who have oodles of vocal self-confidence, maybe relatively unskilled as public speakers.

In a small grouped setting, or even in a larger grouped setting, some people are able to convey their thoughts, ideas, wishes and demands to others better. Those with vocal self-confidence do not necessarily have the best grammar, but it does help.

Some people, by virtue of their size or physical appearance, well-developed muscles, or other distinguishing physical characteristics, seem naturally to catch the attention of others. But the rest of us have to work a little harder.

While there are all kinds of techniques you can use to strengthen your voice and improve your delivery, in the end, the fastest and easiest way to become more vocally self-confident is simply to practice speaking to others in a more confident way. You wanted to hear that, didn't you? I mean, it's a lot easier than having to undergo hours of instruction.

There are simple techniques you can practice right now, especially when there is no one else around to give your vocal cords a good workout.

When you get up in the morning, do you give your voice a workout just as you would work your other muscles? Probably not. I suggest running through the vowels in a harmonic way. Say out loud, Aaaaay, Eeeee, Iiiii, Ooooo, Uuuuu. Then, do it almost as if you're singing them.

Next, try some long words. Out loud, say:

- Discombobulate
- Prestidigitation
- Clavicle
- Philanthropical
- Aphrodisiac

When you've said those a couple times, try some geography:

- Monongahela River

- Mount Kilimanjaro

- Tahiti

- The Susquehanna River

- The Tigris and the Euphrates

- The Mekons Delta

By giving yourself a vocal workout you'll be potentially more expressive all day. Have a warm drink early in the morning. Your vocal chords will thank you. Cold drinks contract the vocal chords, making it harder for you to use them.

If you have a sore or weak voice or throat, try holding your jaw with your hands. Put one hand against your jaw so your fingers touch your ears and your palms are under your chin. This brings immediate warmth to the area and helps to loosen you up.

Also, yawn frequently, especially if you're alone where you can let out a big, loud yawn. Lions yawn all the time, and you don't see anyone ignoring their roar.

It also helps to rotate your shoulders around and around in one direction, then in the alternate direction. Stretches, particularly those where your arms are above your head, can also help.

Orchestra conductors live longer than the average person. Perhaps it's because they keep their hands above their heart; their circulatory systems are strengthened while they work.

Breathing plays an important role in your ability to convey authority on your voice. Don't be afraid to talk breathily on occasion, but don't make it your standard mode of delivery. Sigh when you need to and even hum. The following exercises all help to unlock energy:

- Make gentle out-breaths.

- Hold your breath for a moment, and then suddenly release it.

- Yell. (This one works best when you're alone.)

What part does your lungs play in establishing vocal authority? Strong lungs help achieve more effective breathing. If you're born with strong lungs, thank your lucky stars.

The only thing you can do to potentially improve your lung capacity is swimming. Researchers think that this is because of the increased pressure on your lungs when you are in the water. The way to make your lungs weaker is clear: Exercise in polluted air near carbon monoxide, or in cities where the smog level is high. Also smoke heavily until regular wheezing and coughing becomes natural for you.

You have probably heard this before but few people pay any homage to it. The most effective and efficient breathing is done by using the abdominal muscles rather than the rib cage. Whenever you use your diaphragm (located on the inside of your stomach roughly where your navel is) to do the work instead of your rib muscles, you're far more efficient.

The fastest way to understand diaphragmatic breathing is to lie down on the floor, place your hands over your midsection, and breathe normally. Do you feel your stomach going up and down? That's diaphragmatic breathing, and you can do it while you're standing or sitting.

If you have been talking for a while and you notice that your breathing is shallow, try to bounce a little. Let your knees unlock and go up and down just an inch or so. A mild bounce actually helps you engage your diaphragm while you breathe. Hence, you breathe more efficiently, and are able to summon your resources and maintain vocal strength.

Clavicular-shoulder breathing is evident when you raise and lower your collarbones and shoulders as you inhale and exhale. This is an inefficient way to breathe.

Too many highly athletic types make the mistake of raising their shoulders as well as expanding their rib cages to draw a strong, deep breath. During the heat of battle when you are racing up and down the basketball court, it makes perfect sense to breathe this way. In fact, you probably have no choice. At a resting pulse rate, athletes would be better off breathing using the diaphragm only.

Sit-ups and crunches are helpful for abdominal conditioning, but you also need to give these muscles aerobic conditioning on a regular basis. What is the single best aerobic exercise? Walking.

Have you ever received a phone call from someone you haven't heard from in years? Although they may have not announced who they were, you knew instantly who it was even after only hearing few words.

Like your fingerprints, your voice is unique. Yes, some people sound quite a bit like others, just like some fingerprints are close to others, but they are all different.

Your voice has "music" to it. This is defined by how loudly or softly you speak, whether your pitch rises or falls at the end of sentences, and other characteristics such as richness, texture, and timbre.

What about lower tones? What you may have heard is true. Those who use the lower end of their voice range tend to appear more self-confident. Why?

- Low pitch equates to being in control of your emotions and the situation you face.

- High pitch conveys excitement and possibly fear, insecurity, or nervousness.

Experts say that vocal variety is the key to being an interesting conversationalist and someone to whom others will pay attention. If you want to convey high energy, you can actually tone down your pitch a notch or two. Contrary to Hollywood movies and most TV sitcoms, loud booming voices and ranting and raving behavior grates on your listeners' nerves after a while.

Here are some quick but effective tips for improving your speech:

- Use vocal variety for a more interesting presentation.

- To convey more energy, tone down your pitch a notch.

- Use broad sweeping gestures and a booming voice in moderation. These begin to wear on the audience.

- Tape yourself while practicing your presentation. Then play it back and critique yourself.

- Eliminate "um," "uh," and "er." They add nothing to your communications.

- When you need vocal strength, a mild bounce right where you're standing will summon your resources.

- Keep your jaw relaxed as you speak.

The proof is in the pudding, or if you're a Fried Green Tomatoes fan, the secret is in the sauce. You'll know you've achieved a notable level of vocal self-confidence when you get in front of others and they:

1. Tell you that you're a new and improved you.

2. Do what you say with a lot less resistance.

Now, let's cover a few fundamentals of how to be more effective every time you open your mouth.

It's not what is said, it's how it's said

Any audience you're speaking to, whether it's a party of one or one thousand make an assessment on you from different levels, not only on what you say, but how you say it. Hence, you want to open your part of the conversation or presentation with authority. Communicate with your eyes that you're in control.

Let your audience know that you're speaking to them, not to your notes, the back of the room, the microphone, or the ceiling. Try to be as relaxed and comfortable in front of any group. The vocally self-confident person has the magical ability to be themselves, whether speaking with one person or many in a group.

In front of a larger group, any gestures you use need to be larger. The pauses between your sentences need to be a tad longer. Convey your message with your eyes, mouth, body, and heart. To be at your influential best, stand erect with your best posture. A stiff body, clenched fists, or unanimated expression makes it tough for your listeners to be on your side as they follow along with you.

Appeal to your audience's emotions and intellect, but primarily to their emotions. If you're not naturally animated, work on your facial expressions, gestures, and movement about the podium. If you are naturally animated, thank your lucky stars, but keep trying to improve on how you can better use your vocal talent.

Start with small groups, perhaps speaking to a neighbor, co-worker, staff member, or even your spouse. On each occasion, try to master one new element of advancing your vocal authority. Your first time, perhaps try to fully pronounce the "ing" at the end of each word.

Then you can practice being comfortable with pausing between sentences, and, perhaps another time, use some dramatic hand gestures that are outside of your normal repertoire. No one will know what you are doing, but they will begin to notice the difference in your effectiveness.

Advanced exercises

Here are some advanced exercises to improve your speech:

- To improve your diction, practice speaking with marbles in your mouth, or with a pencil sideways. Also practice intentionally over-enunciating.

- Use exercises to elongate your speaking channel. For example, stick your tongue all the way out, all the way up, left, right, on your back molars as if you're trying to swallow peanut butter, and roll forward.

- Try tongue-twisters to get good at handling lots of words. You know, the old "Peter Piper picked a peck of pickled peppers."

- Practice speaking while dribbling a basketball or engaging in some other physical activity.

- Practice speaking loudly and softly.

- Practice giving certain words emphasis.

So…

- Vocal self-confidence tells others that you are confident and in control.

- To improve your level of vocal self-confidence, practice in front of the mirror, with the camcorder rolling, or with an audiocassette recorder.

- You can strengthen your vocal chords much as you can strengthen muscles in your body. Practice saying long words, melodious words, vowel sounds, and consonant combinations such as "st," "ch," "sp," and "sh."

- Practice in front of real-life subjects as well, starting with one-on-one situations and small groups.

- Find a speech pattern you can live with and which is influential to others, and you can stay with it for a lifetime.

2. The Importance of self-confidence

Let's jump right into some specific strategies you can use to build your self-confidence unfailingly, naturally, and easily.

Rome wasn't built in a day. You've heard that before? How about this: The Chicago Bulls didn't win a championship in their first six seasons that Michael Jordan played. Happily, it won't take you seven years to develop more self-confidence. You actually can see results in as little as seven days, even more in 21 days, and magnificent results within a few months.

Suppose you're a salesperson and have a territory that you cover by car. How much improvement can you make on your presentations if you spend few minutes more in the car carefully collecting your thoughts, perhaps reviewing or rearranging your notes, taking a few deep breaths, and contemplating how you would like the encounter to unfold?

Do you realize that many of the world's top income earners, even years into professional selling, still spend significant amount of time preparing before each sales call?

In many respects, what these top producers are doing is simply going over the basics. They know that preparation, even a few minutes worth, is worth its weight in gold in terms of boosting self-confidence.

This is what propels top performers all over the world. Olympic athletes, major league baseball players, chess masters, you name it. At the beginning of each season or each contest, they all spend the time reviewing or practicing the fundamentals. It's the mediocre performers who think they can skip vital steps. They get bored, or they assume that they're naturally be performing at their best.

While practice doesn't always make perfect, practice does help you increase performance in every endeavor.

You may have noticed that self-confident people seem to resonate an inner calm. Even in a crisis situation, they appear to have a sense of equanimity that impacts every aspect of their lives.

The best athletes play with fire and intensity while maintaining an air of relaxation. By staying focused and relaxed, you can empty your mind of distractions and hence increase your ability to perform, regardless of the task at hand.

Equanimity is the ability to maintain balance and perspective, even in the face of turmoil.

Extending yourself for the express purpose of impressing others runs counterproductive to the notion of self-confidence. You end up spending more time and energy doing things simply because you want to impress others. There's certainly nothing wrong with doing things t occasionally to impress others. The question then; do you have a choice?

The self-confident person engages in such activities. He recognizes that he's most likely to succeed in the things that he enjoys doing, and as the situation dictates, he looks for ways to include others.

Trust others

Few individuals make it in society without the help and support of others. Even if you're an entrepreneur, there are many times throughout the days and weeks when you need to rely on others.

The self-confident person in a work setting delegates freely and easily, but also carefully and methodically. He or she knows that the confidence placed in others helps create a victorious circle, wherein both parties bolster each other's confidence.

Perhaps the saddest people you may know are those who cannot place trust in others. They vehemently cling to whatever projects, information, or good fortune that come their way. They neither share nor benefit from the synergy that could occur from letting others into their "private" domain.

The great leaders of the world, some of the most self-confident people among us, are able to engender a loyal following because they trust people. The greater the trust, the greater the following.

If you win small victories all day long and acknowledge them as such, your subconscious will begin to believe that you are indeed a winner. After all, you rack up victories every day.

Before you discount this as some type of self-congratulatory system, consider that since the subconscious makes no assessment about the magnitude of your victories. Whether the accomplishment is large or small, you set in motion the internal apparatus that will increase the probability of you achieving even more.

Reward yourself

When you do something great, take some time off not only to acknowledge yourself, but to do something nice for yourself. Stop by and get an ice-cream cone or go to the movie you've been wanting to see.

Self-confident people understand the vital importance of enjoying their successes.

If you treat each day and each event as just part of the job or one of many responsibilities, all days begin to look the same. What are some good activities and events for which you can have at least a mini-celebration? The list is very long. Try these for openers. When you:

- Complete a report prior to the deadline

- Are under budget this quarter

- Finish three strokes under your handicap

- Complete your taxes

- Clean out and organize your garage

- Drop those six pounds you've been seeking to shed

- Finally decide to book that vacation in Martinique

Mistakes

Everyone makes mistakes by the boatload, but confident people don't let mistakes drag them down. They don't dwell on them. They regard them as life lessons that give them insights that perhaps they did not have before. If only life was nothing but victories…

Cut yourself some slack. Give yourself some leeway to make mistakes on occasion and be far less than perfect, especially when it comes to being self-confident.

Life repeats itself until you learn the lesson, and then you move on. If you hardly ever made any major mistakes or only made very tiny ones, then that would be a sign that you probably weren't attempting anything worthwhile in life.

After all, if you play it safe, hardly taking your foot off first base, you'll never get picked off, but you won't score many runs either.

Conjure up the image of someone you know who is self-confident. Does he go to pieces when he makes a mistake? Does he get bogged down in when things didn't go right, or does he learn from his mistake and moved on?

Going a step beyond

Self-confident people are not afraid to use their imaginations. They've come to draw upon imagination as a creative, visual, internal rehearsal of what can be. Consider this - how often does stuff just fall into your lap? Do good fortunes just fall into your lap? I'm guessing far less than you would expect it to happen.

Conversely, when you at least contemplated the possibilities, things have a way of working out for the best. Those who lack confidence are afraid to engage their imaginations thinking they will be penalized for wishing for a positive outcome

A philosopher once said, "The imagination is the workshop of the mind." Visualization is one of the many tools of imagination. Here are some ideas to imagine your way to greater self-confidence:

- Imagine yourself giving an effective presentation to your team on Wednesday.

- Imagine yourself going up to someone you're attracted to and easily initiating a conversation.

- Imagine marching into your boss's office and, in a relaxed and confident manner, discussing why it's time for you to receive a raise.

- Imagine the press eagerly writing down what you have to say.

- Imagine being self-confident whenever you choose to be.

If you could rearrange your life so that you were surrounded by self-confident people, and human nature being what it is, eventually you'd become more like them.

Unfortunately, it's not likely you can structure your life to be around self-confident people all the time. You have got to interact with people from all parts of the behavioral spectrum.

Therefore, if you remain confident and know the distinctions between his or her behavior and that of others, you may just be among the lucky few who awake up one bright morning and find that they too are highly self-confident people.

So…

- Practice nearly every day the many simple strategies for increasing your self-confidence.

- Prepare, prepare, prepare. The most accomplished among us keep returning to the basics.

- Look for the small victories as well as the large in everything you do, and reward yourself often.

- Don't dwell on your mistakes, but learn from them and then move on.

- Use your imagination to devise scenarios in which you act in ways that you normally don't allow yourself.

- Hang around, observe, and imitate self-confident people. Self-confidence leaves clues.

3. Money, Money, Money

If you're the eldest child in your family, supposedly, you are inclined to be more self-confident. This may be true sometimes, but not across the board. I've even heard that if you are from an affluent family, you tend to be more self-confident than someone from less well-to-do origins.

Let's take a brief tour to see if these notions hold water.

From Little Orphan Annie to Richie Rich, an age-old question persists: What advantages are there to being raised in an affluent environment? More specifically, is there a link between wealth and self-esteem? Are rich people wealthy because they are self-confident? Does someone who was raised in affluence tend to become assertive?

It appears that self-esteem does indeed lead to wealth. Dennis Waitely, who from the early 1970s to the early 1990s studied wealthy, successful, high achievers from all walks of life, found a strong correlation between a strong vocabulary and greater income-producing potential. This doesn't mean that merely having an extensive vocabulary or being verbose add up to self-esteem or wealth.

Brilliant Ph.D.s may speak poetically on one topic and give an extended philosophical discourse on another, but they may not be self-confident. A good vocabulary, however, certainly helps. The natural ability to speak up is a valuable skill. In addition, the self-confident tend to rise faster in their careers and, yes, it will earn them more money.

Within professional service firms, the "finders," people who go out and create new businesses, earn much more than the "minders" who manage the projects, and the "grinders" who actually do the work. In large organizations, the people who make themselves heard rise to the top.

Some of the very wealthy asserted themselves at a young age. Whatever else you may think of him, Henry Ross Perot is an excellent example of someone from humble origins. Short of stature, Ross Perot, by virtue of his self-esteem, generated nearly incalculable wealth.

Perot grew up in the Depression era. At age 12, he approached the circulation manager of his town newspaper, the Gazette, and offered to deliver newspapers to people's homes in the poverty-stricken area of town. No one had ever conceived of this idea - the prevailing assumption was that poor people could not afford, let alone read, a newspaper. Perot felt otherwise.

Within a short period Perot was making so much money by delivering newspapers that his commission was in jeopardy of being reduced. Never one to sit back and let others control his destiny, Perot wrote to the publisher and complained about how he was being treated by the paper's management after making so much money for the paper. The publisher agreed with him and he was able to continue the lucrative arrangement he had set up.

While working for IBM and becoming their top sales representative, Perot conceived of initiating a service branch within IBM that would help clients learn how to use and apply office technology to improve their business operations.

IBM declined to follow through on his idea, and Perot, at age 31, decided to leave his high-commission-earning job to start his own company, EDS. In 1984, he sold EDS to General Motors for $2.5 billion, and in 1986 sold his remaining stock in the company for $700 million. In one move after another, Perot asserted himself on the way to his ultimate prosperity.

Consider Kavelle R. Bajaj, who came to the United States from India in 1974 and faced cultural and gender barriers. In her conservative Indian upbringing, Bajaj was expected to place family affairs over a career. She opened a small business selling imported goods, but almost immediately became dissatisfied and disappointed in this venture.

Eventually she opted to try again. In the early 1980s, following the breakup of American Telephone and Telegraph, Bajaj borrowed $5,000 and took computer and database management classes at a nearby college. She then started a company called I-Net, which provided telecommunication contracting services primarily to the Department of Defense.

The company developed a solid reputation and grew quickly, if not evenly, over the next several years. In 1990, Bajaj landed a $100-million long-term contract from the Air Force for computer systems engineering and software. Bajaj attributes her success to initiative, self-esteem, and commitment to ideals. "There is opportunity in the United States for the person who wants to make it," she says. "There is no reason to make excuses."

The ways and the means

If self-esteem leads to wealth, does wealth lead to self-esteem? Those who are wealthy have the means to make their wishes more readily known than those who are not as wealthy. If you're wealthy, perhaps you have more time to be in organizations and take leadership positions. Certainly, someone who is wealthy has more options in life than someone who is not.

Historically, men have been heads of nations, leaders of governments, generals, warriors, orators, debaters, professors, and scholars. They were more likely to be published and celebrated. Male children emulated their fathers, while female children emulated their mothers. Once again, however, your ability to be self-confident, whether you're a man or a woman, is dependent mostly on the unique and particular aspects of your own situation.

Everything that you've encountered in this book, including this chapter, shows that you can learn to be more self-confident, regardless of whatever potential disadvantages, impediments, or obstacles may be in your path. In fact, you can look for small victories in everyday life that will enhance your ability to be assertive.

4. Body Language

In this chapter, we'll explore what physical self-esteem is all about and how you can project it. You don't necessarily need to run to the gym and pick up the barbells. Instead, you'll merely learn how to know when you're in control.

Physical self-esteem is the ability to convey with your body with demeanor and that you can stand up for yourself and be in charge.

If you had the chance to speak to the police department in your community, you'll find out that they have at least a loose profile of the typical victim of a mugging. Independent of sex and age, those most prone to be attacked:

- Walk with shoulders slumped forward.

- Look down.

- Have poor posture.

- Seem unaware of the larger surroundings.

Conversely, independent of sex and age, those less likely to be targets of muggings exhibit at least a few, if not, all of the following characteristics:

- Walk with an even stride.

- Keep their heads up.

- Take in much, if not all of their surroundings.

- Take the seat of your choice.

- Maintain a good posture.

- Dress well.

- Prepare.

- Smile.

- Maintain a pleasant demeanor.

- Speak at an even and unhurried pace.

- Firmly shake hands.

- Take the initiative to greet the other party.

- Remain in control during the meeting.

- Deliver your points with gusto.

- Leave at the appropriate time.

- Stride out with vigor.

What about the time when you were a shrinking violet, not at your best? What can you recall about the messages that you imparted, either verbally or nonverbally?

Do you recall that you:

- Didn't look the other party right in the eye?

- Didn't speak with authority?

- Weren't confident entering the room?

- Didn't take the seat of your choice?

- Didn't maintain good posture?

- Weren't dressed well?

- Weren't prepared?

- Didn't smile?

- Didn't maintain a pleasant demeanor?

- Didn't firmly shake hands?

- Didn't take the initiative to greet the other party?

- Didn't remain in control during the meeting?

- Didn't deliver your points with gusto?

- Didn't leave at the appropriate time?

- Didn't stride out with vigor?

Now, for the Illinois Lotto Jackpot, here's your question: What was the difference between the time when you were your dynamic self projecting physical self-esteem and the time when you were your wimp? Chances are you felt confident in the situations in which you projected well, and experienced a lack of confidence in situations where you came off as a douche bag.

Body language is critical in establishing a positive image

Body language certainly accounts for a sizable chunk of the message you impart to others. The simple key to projecting an aura of greater physical self-esteem is self-awareness. When you're aware of what your body imparts to others, the changes you need to make come naturally.

It's not mandatory for you to hit the gym, but you don't see too many couch potatoes who are physically self-confident. Even the mildest exercise will help you stay in reasonable physical shape, and hence help you to project to others. If you belong to a health club or a gym, you undoubtedly know that a variety of weight machines are available today that can help you work out virtually any muscle group in your body.

Health professionals say that working out for as little as 30 minutes, three times a week is sufficient to give you vim and vigor.

Free weights and various pulley machines are available in most health clubs or gyms. Many of the exercises with weights help strengthen your upper body, which in turn helps your posture. When you're able to throw your chest out and your shoulders back naturally as you walk, you breathe more efficiently, stand up straighter, tire less easily, and appear more confident.

Why do some people command your respect, even when they say nothing to you or do nothing in particular? Beyond how you carry yourself, and how your body moves, many other factors contribute to your physical self-esteem. Let's review each of these briefly; keeping an eye on ways you can convey the kind of message to others that you want to.

Facial expression

Do you go around smiling all day? Do you frown or scowl? Those facial expressions convey messages; a blank expression conveys little. If you have a blank expression on your face, no matter what you're saying, the other party will have a hard time "hearing you" and look for other clues, such as your body language and voice, to get your overall message.

If you're the person with the blank expression, this may explain why it often appears that no one is listening to you. Use your face to express meaning!

Voice strength and quality

Are you among the masses that ramble, mumble, or otherwise truncate words? Are you normally soft spoken, particularly when you need more vocal power to convey your message? Many people have particular problems with using their voices when it comes to meeting a stranger, speaking to others over the telephone, or speaking to a group.

If you know someone who frequently speaks to you with a blank expression, you now know why you find yourself consistently drifting off when this person speaks to you. You'll have to engage all of your listening skills to gain a fuller meaning of their message.

Posture

Regarding posture, mentally review how you go about your day. Do you sit up straight in your chair, or are you frequently slumped over? Is your chair at the proper height for you to use on your desk, computer, telephone, and other equipment? When conversing with others, say, in the hallway, do you frequently lean on the wall or a table, or do you stand erect and relaxed?

Eye contact

Whether you're speaking to someone or listening, your use of eye contact says a lot about you. Looking at someone only intermittently, looking past him or looking down at the floor is a much less effective means of keeping him in the conversation and having him heed what you say.

Instead, maintain more extended eye contact. I'm not talking about staring somebody down, fixating on him to the point where you don't ever turn away. That can be considered rude and disconcerting, among other things. I am talking about holding your eye contact for at least three to five seconds at some point and as long as 20 to 25 seconds at others.

You can break this up by nodding occasionally, briefly looking up at the ceiling or down at the floor when you're trying to recall something or come up with a point, pointing to a chalkboard or document between you, or simply glancing away for a moment in any direction.

Think about the times when you had a conversation with someone who avoided eye contact with you at all costs:

- Was this person influential?

- Did their words have the most impact possible?

- Did you feel comfortable about the conversation?

Chances are, you answered no in all three cases. Others may feel the same if they are in conversation with you and your eyes are everywhere except on them.

Use of gestures

Gestures help those around you understand what you're trying to convey. If you're like most people, you're probably unaware of the gestures you use when speaking to others. Some gestures help you make your point and win the attention and respect of others.

Other gestures, including those you probably impart unconsciously, can actually detract from your message and say, "I don't really intend to follow up on this," or "I don't intend to hold you accountable."

A lot of misinformation about what some gestures mean has been handed down over the years. For example, dozens if not hundreds of books suggest that if someone's arms are folded across his chest, he's conveying defensiveness and appearing closed to the information being presented. This could be true on occasion, but it is largely hogwash. A person might fold his arms across his chest for a number of reasons, including the following:

- He might be cold, and crosses his arms and hands across his chest for warmth.

- He might be bored but still not defensive.

- He might simply feel comfortable with his hands in that position.

Certainly, any fidgeting, nervous tapping, or other involuntary gestures you display repeatedly may distract the other party and diminish the impact of your message. We've all been in conversation with someone who taps their foot, fidgets with a pen or pencil, or frequently scratches their ear. Most likely, these types of gestures do not add to that person's interpersonal effectiveness, but detract from it.

Moving in too close to someone can be as ineffective as pulling away from them. Many people don't like to have someone, "in their face," and may get defensive or feel threatened. This will detract from their ability to actually hear you, and they may capitulate in the short run, not adding to a climate of respect or trust.

Here are some vocal detractors, the presence of which will diminish the impact of your message, followed by the antidotes:

- Stiff or formal speech

Antidote: Spice up your language, use contractions, put down your notes.

- Gross mispronunciation of words, particularly common words

Antidote: Use a dictionary to look up words and practice using them before uttering to others.

- Overuse of clichés, slang, and hackneyed expressions

Antidote: Listen to yourself on tape and pick out overused expressions. Also ask others if you overuse some phrases.

- Use of non-sequiturs

Antidote: Stick to the main point; don't ramble.

- Overuse of filler language, such as "um," "er," "ah," "you see," and "you know"

Antidote: Give yourself more time between sentences. Get comfortable with pausing in silence between phrases or thoughts instead of relying on "um," "er." "ah," and "you know" types of unnecessary connectors.

- Lack of clarity

Antidote: Think about the point of your message in advance.

- Failure to come to a coherent point

Antidote: Have your strong point ready. Mentally rehearse it before speaking.

Vocal self-esteem

We all know people who are vocally self-confident but not physically self-confident. These are people who, by virtue of their positions, demand you pay attention to them. One of these people may be your boss, or some bureaucrat who speaks with authority but never gets out of his chair.

It is possible to have physical self-esteem without vocal self-esteem. Generally, however, the two go hand in hand. Someone who has good posture, stands tall, uses gestures appropriately, and makes sufficient eye contact has the best chance of being heard.

When you combine physical self-esteem with vocal self-esteem, also known as vocal authority, you're cooking with gas heat. It helps if you have a rich, deep, bass voice, but if you don't, take heart. Millions of people all over the planet who are far less than rich still manage to have vocal authority. It's all a matter of how you use your voice.

You want to employ vocal variety and engage your listeners - let them know that you're speaking to them without undivided attention.

Over the years, much has been written about walking your talk. I'd like to introduce, for the first time in this universe, the importance of talking your walk - using your voice in a manner that connotes vocal self-esteem and is consistent with the physical self-esteem you may also display.

Walking your talk is a worn-out cliché that essentially means you personally live up to what you talk about; that is, you practice what you preach.

If you are able to talk your walk, you have the best of both worlds. Everything about you says, "When I speak, there's a good chance it's worth listening to."

So…

- Conveying physical self-esteem is based less on your size, weight, or muscles and more on how you carry and project yourself.

- You convey alertness and awareness to others mainly through your eyes.

- You don't have to exercise to convey strength or authority.

- Effective use of gestures helps the other party stay attuned to what you're saying.

- Being both physically and vocally self-confident gets others to listen and respond to you.

5. Spouse and Children

In his book, Care of the Soul, Thomas Moore says that human beings are "infinitely complicated and profound." He observes that our family relationships might be good or not so good, but in either case, we may understand them better if we acknowledged more often just how complicated and profound other members of our family can be. Many of our family members have a history that we'll never know; that is, a history that they've created during the time they were away from us.

Moore also suggests that instead of trying to diagnose or predict the behavior of our spouse, parents, or children, we can better spend our time appreciating them for who and what they are. This would undoubtedly improve family relations.

We've all experienced firsthand the rigors of attempting to be self-confident within your immediate family. Do you find yourself falling into familiar communication patterns when interacting with members of your family when you try to get them to do something or to make a point?

Perhaps a major impediment to being self-confident within your family is the sheer proximity of your family members. It's easy to fall into the mindset that you know all about them because you see them so frequently - what their views are, how they'll respond, what sets them off, and how you set them off.

You tell your child to straighten up his room and you notice he barely lifts a finger. You raise your voice, and he moves a little faster.

You come back in a few minutes, and perhaps he is dawdling again. You re-emphasize what you want him to do. Now, however, you sound like your parents when they talked that way to you 28 years ago.

Perhaps you're having a discussion with your spouse about where you want to go on your next vacation. Your spouse says the mountains, and you say the shore. You present your case; your spouse presents her case. Neither side really listens so the conversation degenerates into a spat.

You may realize you've been down this trail before. Once you become a little heated, the argument takes on a life of its own. The net effect is you are anything but self-confident.

A growing body of evidence suggests that to be effective with members of your immediate family, or anyone else for that matter, you need to connect with that other person so that she actually thinks you're on her side. In other words, to achieve the outcome in your favor, you need to help the other person achieve the outcome they are looking for.

There's no need to think that every interpersonal encounter you have with members of your family hereafter means you have to go out of your way to help them achieve something in a tit-for-tat manner. Sometimes the other party needs only to gain a sense of respect, attention, caring, or some other feeling that you can impart while asserting yourself.

When you engage in tit-for-tat behavior with someone, you match the magnitude and frequency of the other person's actions.

If you're like many people, you may need to let your internal engine rev down after work before interacting with your family. After all, you're not talking to Joe in accounting, Sally in marketing, Hal in logistics, or Jennifer in the Springfield division anymore.

Here's a quick quiz to help remind you that professional self-esteem is not the same as self-esteem in your family. Before making your wishes known at home...

- Have you taken three deep breaths?

- Do you exchange pleasantries?

- Do you ask your spouse or children how their day went?

- Do you make eye contact and speak face-to-face?

- Do you give your complete and undivided attention?

- Do you use polite and complimentary language?

- Do you offer praise or acknowledgment for something other family members have done?

- Have you pitched in on some household task or chore?

Here's how to score your answers. If you answered "yes" to seven or more of the above, you're probably fooling yourself. If you answered "yes" four to six times, your family will probably be responsive to you. If you answered "yes" three times or less, you need to take immediate action. Review the list again and decide which five gestures you'll employ tomorrow after work.

If you are a gung-ho, career-climbing world-beater, arriving home still mentally immersed in the affairs of the workday, members of your family may have difficulty relating to you, let alone heeding you.

Your spouse

Is it harder today to be in a marriage or a relationship than in previous eras? It's an issue I won't explore in detail, but undoubtedly you have some opinions about this. In an era in which divorce rates are high and some domestic quarrels make the evening news, it's safe to say that it's difficult for many spouses to interact effectively with one another these days.

Open any number of women's or men's magazines, and you'll find that communicating with one's partner is at the top of the list in articles on relationship problems.

Thomas Moore says that each marriage have its own identity, direction, and movement. It takes on a life beyond the original intentions of either spouse. Because the roots of any spousal interaction (including any argument) may go back to the very start of the relationship, marriages or other intimate relationships may well be the toughest relationships to keep vibrant and on an even keel.

When you know your spouse is willing to really listen to you, and vice versa, you can both be more effective at resolving differences of perspective or opinion. Besides drawing on everything you've learned up to this point, here's an extensive checklist of behaviors and communication techniques you may wish to use on your next encounter:

- Minimize any negative feelings you have before speaking.

- Eliminate the notion that your partner "should have done this" or "could have done that."

- Contemplate how he/she might view the issue you're about to discuss.

- Let go of feelings of omniscience or superiority.

- Realize that your way may be the way this time, but it's not always so.

- Look for the good in your partner.

- Consider things to appreciate rather than issues to analyze.

Once you engage in conversation, especially if there is a chance that the conversation might get heated, your challenge to remain self-confident becomes even greater. If you recall and employ even a few of the following interpersonal communication techniques, you're bound to have more favorable results:

Start your sentences with the following phrases:

"I would enjoy having ..."

"I would prefer if..."

"I would appreciate it if..."

"I like it when you ..."

"Could you please ..."

"I need your help in ..."

"I'm hoping you'll..."

"Would you join me in ..."

"Could you get me ..."

"It would really be helpful if..."

Use feeling words more often than thinking words:

"I feel as if we ..." rather than "I think we ..."

The world is full of lonely people who won most of the arguments but lost the war. They were the dominating communication partner but ended up losing their relationship.

Make requests; don't issue orders:

"Could you ..."

"Would you ..."

"Will you ..."

"My request is that you ..."

Often, a brief statement of empathy before making a request helps soften any assertion you might make. For example:

"I need to request something of you ..."

"I can see you've been working hard ..."

"I know you wanted to relax today..."

"There's something I need to ask you ..."

"I need your attention for three minutes ..."

"Could I steal you away for a moment?"

"Let's sit down for a moment..."

Here are some gestures and statements to avoid because they'll reduce your chances of being self-confident. For example:

- Any of the unassertive phrases such as, "Let me repeat myself"

- Blaming language, such as, "It's your fault that..." or judgmental language, such as, "I think it was a bad idea for you to ..."

- Demanding language, such as, "Pay attention ..."

- Accusatory language, such as, "What's going on here ..."

- Abrasive language, such as, "Look, I only have a minute ..."

- Domineering language, such as, "I already told you ..."

Also, when asking a question, avoid language in which you apologize, such as, "I'm sorry to bother you with this, but . . . ," or ask for permission, such as, "May I ask you a quick question?" People often believe they are softening their request, but it makes a person sound unsure or timid.

As you engage in give-and-take dialog, depending on the situation and where the conversation is heading, use one or more of the following modes of conversation:

- Support the others' viewpoint, with phrases such as, "I think I understand where you're coming from..."

- Acknowledge the other person's non-vocal response by saying, "I know what I'm saying may come as a surprise..."

- Allow for other possibilities, such as, "I know you may see this differently..."

- Offer periodic praise, such as, "You've been good about this, bear with me for one more minute ...

- Offer links between points, such as, "So you see, adding A to B, I figure ..."

Obviously, I can't give you the vocal nuances that would make each of these phrases work as intended. Even if you used any one of them magnificently, that would not guarantee success. Still, using this kind of language in an engaging interpersonal manner will help enormously in many situations.

Because being confident with a spouse or other people is special, you may have to extend yourself even further than what I've just covered. I mean, hey, you're going to have endless conversations that involve some form of give-and-take. So, periodically try some approaches that help grease the skids.

Admit when you're wrong

I don't know anyone who really likes to do this, but doing it on occasion creates an environment in which you keep your credibility at a nice, high level. If you've ever known anyone who always insists they're right, you know how infuriating it is when such a person approaches you with yet another issue, especially when their position is once again questionable.

By freely acknowledging your own fallibility, you project yourself as a more balanced, rational, reasonable person.

Everyone is fallible - that is, subject to goofing, making errors, or in general being wrong about something.

Who would be more influential with you? Someone who thinks they are always right or someone who asserts himself for what he wants, but acknowledges he might make mistakes along the way?

Keep it light

Sometimes, when making a request of a stern nature, your body language, posture, and demeanor don't need to be stern. If you play heavy all the time, especially when making requests of others who regularly comply with your requests, they will regard being around you as burdensome.

Your children

What's the matter with kids today? Probably nothing more than what was the matter with kids of the previous generation.

I'm not a child psychologist, and chances are you aren't either. Neither of us needs to be one, however, when it comes to being self-confident with our children. If you treat your children as full-fledged human beings from the time they are small, they'll respond to you in ways only previously imagined.

You can be much more self-confident when you say some things with a smile or a twinkle in your eye, because the other party finds your approach so much more palatable.

Lording over someone, even if that someone happens to be your child, is rarely as effective as being self-confident with them in the short run, and it never is in the long run. You can, however, employ all of the ideas about self-esteem that you learn in this book with your children.

Treating your children like full-fledged human being don't mean treat them like adults. They are, however, individuals with their own sets of likes and dislikes, perceptions, and notions about the world.

When you speak to another person in your office or around town, do you use language that is similar to the following:

- "Because I know what's best for you ..."

- "Because I said so ..."

- "I don't want to say it again ..."

- "If I have to ask you one more time…"

- "If I have to tell you one more time ..."

- "Never mind what I do ..."

Hopefully, the answer to my question above is that you never use such language with other adults. Why? It simply wouldn't work. They'd look at you, roll their eyes, and tell you to get off it, and that's the most polite language they might use.

Why, then, would you believe that using such language would be effective with your children? Is it because you:

- Heard it from your own parents?

- Saw it on television?

- Believe your child is not intelligent?

- Heard something about tough love and think you're dispensing it?

- Don't know how else to make a request?

Your assignment is to forever banish unassertive communication patterns with your children to the far corner of the universe.

The statements above use unassertive language and demotivate people. They do not prompt action, inspire others, or leave the other party feeling good about the interaction.

Don't let any minor or temporary "success" you think you achieved cloud your view. You might be winning battles, but you'll be losing the war. Anyone who is confronted with such language may concede and bow to your demands, but they do so begrudgingly. The last thing you need to create is a rebel in your own family. You have enough problems already!

Okay, you ask, how do I get little Justin or Kristen to respond to my requests?

Here, in order and without adornment, is composite advice from leading child psychologists and authors on what your child wants and needs.

Receiving these items on a regular basis will make your child more than willing to capitulate to your requests most of the time - by golly, the first time you ask!

- Love your children and demonstrate it. Love may not conquer all, but it conquers a lot.

Do you go out of your way to do things for the people you love? When you love your children, they tend to love you back and honor much more of what you request.

- Spend some time with your children each day. I don't care how hectic it gets at work, what your responsibilities are, or what your life is like in general.

A lot of rubbish has been written in the last two decades about the importance of spending "quality" time with your children. What exactly is the lack of quality time - junk time? Given the choice between spending an hour with you in less than the best circumstances and five minutes of "quality" time with you, I assure you most children will choose the hour. To them, quantity equals quality in many regards.

If you simply bop in and out of their rooms or in and out of their lives, however, the likelihood that you can be self-confident with them logically diminishes.

All the time you spend with your children can be quality time, even if you're only watching an inane television show. There are always things you can explain, conversation you can initiate during the commercials, and little tidbits of communication that go back and forth all show long.

- Constantly reinforce your children's behavior. Kids are approval and attention machines; at least they start out that way. Nine-tenths or more of what they do is either to get your approval or your attention. If you withhold your approval, they try even harder to get it. If you continue to withhold it, they give up in time and settle for getting your attention. The problem is that they may get your attention in ways you might not enjoy.

In terms of getting your children to listen and respond to you, this means that you can begin right now, today, even if your relationship with your children is somewhat strained. You can get them to listen and respond by "rewarding them" when they do things you want them to do.

Do you want your child to clean his room? The next time he cleans his room as well as every other time, offer responses such as the following:

"You've done a wonderful job here. Congratulations."

"Your room looks sparkling. You've done well."

"What a pleasure to walk into such a clean bedroom."

"I'm pleased to see the fine job you've done here."

"I love it when you clean your room."

"Excellent. Excellent job!"

It's of no avail to comment three days later what a wonderful job your child did cleaning his room. Why? If you're verbal, gestural, or material reward trails the performance over too great a time interval, the mental and emotional connection is lost.

In addition to your words, let your body language express your glee as well. Widen your eyes. Perk up. Smile. Convey your joy, pleasure, and rapture for your child's efforts in cleaning his room. You practically cannot overdo this. Even if you think it's not working, your support has a cumulative effect.

Each time you reward a child through gestures or verbal acknowledgment, you add to the probability that he'll clean his room again, more readily after your request. You may even reach the point where he cleans his room without you asking at all; the response he receives is so personally rewarding he cleans his room simply to receive it again.

Rewards

What about giving rewards such as money, a trip to the ice cream store, or staying up late? These items can work. However, the situation is different for everyone. Dr. Aubrey Daniels, in his book Bringing out the Best in People, says that what motivates one person may not motivate another. You have to explore.

You have to specifically find out what works best for your child. However, this much is clear: Regardless of the reward you offer, it must closely follow the performance.

What kind of language can you use to make a point when your child looks forward to cleaning his or her room or honoring any other request that you make? Try some of these on for size, noting that none of this is parent-to-child language. Rather, this is person-to-person language. You're treating your child as a fully functioning human being, albeit a younger, smaller, less knowledgeable, or less-experienced version of an adult.

- "I'd like you to clean up your room now."

- "It's important that you finish your homework by seven. Please get started on it in the next couple of minutes."

- "It's okay if you don't want to finish all your vegetables, but I'd like you to eat at least half of them."

- "Would you prefer to take out the garbage or dry the dishes?"

- "You can stay out until 9:30 p.m., but no later. This is a school night.

The eldest child

The eldest child in the family has different characteristics than those of succeeding children. For example, among many, the eldest child tends to be more adventurous. She may be inclined to travel more; live further from her original, nuclear home; and take more risks personally and socially.

In cases where the eldest child is put in charge of the other children, the child might have had a head start in becoming self-confident. If the eldest child is a female, she, in particular, may have had to practice parental or more specifically, "mommy" skills at an early age.

As I've emphasized throughout, your ability to be self-confident is largely optional. Eldest child or not, you always have the choice to engage in self-confident behavior. Even if you are the youngest in your family, the opportunity to assert yourself is there for the taking.

Rejoice in the little ways that your children assert themselves. They'll need such skills when they get older.

Bossiness

Sometimes it's difficult for children to learn self-esteem. Often, self-esteem in making requests and standing or speaking up for yourself in a way that makes the other person feel good about the interaction slips into the realm of bossiness.

Children are perfect mirrors of our own behavior. All studies show that the habits you engage in are likely to be picked up by your children, whether it's smoking, swearing, driving too fast, or abusing your spouse.

If you boss your children around, not treating them as full-fledged human beings but as your property or chattel, don't be surprised to find them bossing around their siblings or other children. After all, they imitate you, and they're probably doing a good job of it.

Lucy in the "Peanuts" comic strip is the epitome of the bossy personality. Lucy calls people names. She doesn't make requests; she issues demands. There are times when the other kids barely tolerate her. She is the one who causes Charlie Brown to say, "Good grief!" more often than anyone else. If you want your kids to act like Lucy, keep yelling at them, bossing them around, and scold them for when they do not accomplish things.

So…

- To be effective with members of your immediate family, you need to connect with them so that they feel you're on their side.

- Because being self-confident with a spouse or other people is special, you may have to extend yourself even further.

- "Communication problems" is most frequently cited by survey respondents as the top reason for divorces in America.

- Rejoice in the little ways that your children assert themselves. They'll need such skills when they get older.

- Children are perfect mirrors of our own behavior.

6. Parents and other Relatives

Are you among the many people who have longstanding miscommunications with your relatives? By relatives I mean parents, mothers-in-law, fathers-in-law, uncles, cousins, nieces, and nephews, whether they are of the first, second, or once-removed variety. Vast numbers of people have problems in this area. If they didn't, Hollywood movies and endless TV sitcoms wouldn't profit from milking "mother-in-law" scenarios and jokes decade after decade.

In this section, we'll take a look at your ability to be self-confident with different categories of relatives, including your parents, your spouse's parents, uncles and aunts, nieces and nephews, cousins, and other relations, both near and far.

Parents

If you've ever stayed at your parents' home after years of living on your own, undoubtedly you found yourself falling back into familiar communication patterns. Perhaps your parents have house rules that you don't fully agree with. Perhaps they criticize you or nag you, and you respond. Perhaps your communication pattern even reverts back to when you lived there as a child, a teenager, or young adult.

With all the exclamation in the world, you can say, "MOTHER!" or "FATHER!" and your mother or father will give you rapt attention. If your parents are like most parents, tell them that you really have to talk to them, and you've got their attention.

Nevertheless, for many people, being self-confident with their parents is among the easier tasks when it comes to self-esteem. Why? They cut you more slack. They give you more latitude.

The way to get your parents to listen and respond is much the same as you would with your spouse, children, or anyone else you're close to. You can go back and reapply what you've already learned to situations with your parents.

There are a few nuances to asserting yourself with your parents. If you can steer clear of some of these pitfalls, then you greatly enhance your ability to get your parents to listen and respond.

Speak to your parent adult-to-adult. Don't fall into any role you might have played when you were six, 11, or 19. If you revert back to childlike communication with your parents, chances are it will evoke responses from your parents similar to those of the past.

Be secure in your role as an adult, and your parent or parents will have no choice but to respond to you as an adult.

- Avoid being manipulated by guilt. When you call your mother, she answers and says, "Oh, hi. I was so surprised. You hardly ever call anymore!" This is the part where you don't fall for it.

If your mother (or father, just as well) wants you to call more often, she needs to read this book. If she wants you to call more often, each time you call she should say something like:

"It's wonderful to hear from you."

"I'm so happy when you call."

"The sound of your voice is comforting to me."

"How are you doing; I've been thinking about you!"

If you're face-to-face with your parents and they attempt to make you feel guilty, don't respond to it. Suppose your father says, "Is it too much to ask?" If you say yes, you contribute to a climate of potential hostility and hurt feelings. If you say no, you capitulate to his wishes and set yourself up for further manipulation and feelings of guilt another time. What would be a more appropriate response? How about:

"What's the real issue behind all this?"

- Don't allow your parents to offer prolonged criticism. Because they're your parents, they may feel entitled to criticize you, and some criticisms can actually be objective, valid, and even helpful.

It's much too easy to fly off the handle in the face of criticism from your parents, especially when you're an adult. "You never approved of anything that I..." Don't reciprocate with anger or criticize in return.

Instead, assert yourself! The more balanced and even-toned you remain, the more your parents get the message that you're not willing to engage in the same old unproductive behavior patterns anymore.

Tired of being criticized by your parents? Try making a request about how you'd like to discuss the issue. Tell them how you'd like them to offer recommendations that they think might be helpful for you in the future.

In-laws

You'd think the more you get to know your spouse's parents and vice versa, the less potential there is for any misunderstanding. But I have not encountered a study correlating the length of time you know your in-laws with your ability to communicate effectively with them.

Indeed, some people naturally hit it off in a matter of seconds, while others don't seem to connect effectively, even after years of knowing one another.

The possible causes of communicating effectively or being self-confident with your in-laws are as numerous and diverse as personality characteristics among human beings. Here are a few of the possibilities. Perhaps your in-laws:

- Regard you as an outsider, someone who has invaded their nuclear family (even if their son or daughter is a full-fledged adult in society, left their household more than a decade ago, and chose a partner wisely).

- Are insecure about their relationship with their son or daughter and feel you may represent some type of threat to that relationship.

- Never warm up to anybody in their family.

- Have unrealistic expectations about the kind of partner their son or daughter would find in life, and try as you might, you'll never live up to those expectations.

- Can't concede that you had a life before you met their son or daughter and hence, regard you as something less than a fully functioning human being.

- Have always had trouble communicating with their son or daughter and now are extending that inability to include you.

- Subconsciously never wanted their child to marry. After all, that's a signal that they're aging.

- Liked someone else their child dated before you and wanted that person to be part of their family. Thus, anyone who comes after, in their minds, will never completely live up to their expectations.

- Are prejudiced about your background, education, religion, social status, ethnic origin, or some other personal characteristics. There are Archie Bunkers in the world, even though, miraculously, their children sometimes grow up to be nice people.

- Connect you with someone else who made them feel uncomfortable, or they simply don't like your looks.

- Resent compromises their child has made to be in a marital relationship with you. For example, you may have ended up moving far from the in-laws' home, or you're in a profession that demand odd hours or prolonged travel.

- Feel they never see their child enough, and now they will see him or her even less with you in the picture.

- Feel their ability to communicate with their child was unique and special and that anyone else in the "channel" is a distracting or disruptive element.

- Have not had a happy marriage and they project onto your marriage the same misery and misfortune. Thus, without knowing you or attempting to get to know you, they surmise that you will be the cause of such misery for their child.

- Vigorously disapprove some aspect of your life; for example, you have been married before, have children, smoke, drink, have a large dog, or drive a pickup truck, and they have let this single factor cloud their perception of you.

You can see from this extensive list above - and it could have been much longer - that many of the reasons why you may have communication and/or self-esteem problems with your in-laws have little to do with you.

Of course, there are things you could be doing to create the difficult situation - perhaps you expect them to be more like your parents, or blame them for difficulties their child has, and so on. Getting along is a two-way street!

In the book, How to Keep People from Pushing Your Buttons, Dr. Albert Ellis and Dr. Arthur Lang note that the first step in not letting others upset you is to accept the fact that they can behave like "real creeps." This statement doesn't mean that they actually are creeps, but rather that they can behave that way. Moreover, there's nothing particularly wrong in feeling nervous, angry, concerned, guilty, upset, flustered, embarrassed, grief-stricken, displeased, or edgy on occasion, even in the proximity of your in-laws.

The key, say Drs. Ellis and Lang, is to realize that other people don't really control these emotions within us. We're in charge of our emotions that control our lives, and we need to remember that. "When we worry too much about what others think of us or worry too much about getting respect, failing, or making fools of ourselves," we forget we're really the ones in charge of ourselves."

Let's look at a variety of encounters you may have with your in-laws. Keep an eye on how you can assert yourself better.

First, I need to lay down a couple of ground rules. You might want to examine this list closely because these are non-negotiable:

1. You don't have to earn the right to be your spouse's husband or wife. You already did that the day you got married.

2. You're going to have to be forgiving, forgiving, and forgiving. As the late Dr. Norman Cousins once said, "Life is an adventure in forgiveness."

3. Relax. If you are calm and relaxed, you'll be perceived as being more emotionally intelligent, regardless of what else you do. In addition, if you intend to be married for a long time, you'll need this capability.

4. Give up the notion of trying to become what you think your in-laws want you to be.

Okay, now that you've fully absorbed these ground rules, here are some scenarios in which you can be self-confident with your spouse's parents, and still live to eat at their dinner table another day.

The polite decline

You'll undoubtedly be asked to do many things, such as have another portion of some food you cannot stand, spend another two hours with "Dad" tinkering with his car in the garage, or stay far longer at a family function than you can possibly stand.

Assuming that you've spoken with your spouse in advance about your endurance test posed by your in-laws, offer a brief apology and excuse yourself. For example:

"It's been great, but it's getting kind of late."

"I'm sorry. I didn't realize the day was passing by so quickly."

"As much as I'd like to, I simply couldn't force down even another bite."

"Thanks, I'll take a raincheck on that one."

Don't start apologizing left and right for things you are not sorry for, or over choices you've made about your time or level of participation. Do not compromise yourself. Remember the essence of self-esteem:

- Conveying appropriate self-interest
- Maintaining integrity
- Upholding your rights as a person

You can leave me out of this one

Suppose you're drawn into an argument between your spouse and his or her parents or into an argument between the parents themselves. If you don't choose to be part of the encounter, you have a variety of options for bowing out gracefully:

- "I don't have a well-developed opinion in this area and so, won't offer one."
- (Said while smiling) "Sony folks, I'm just not going to be drawn into this."
- "In all honesty, I don't see a part for myself in this particular discussion."
- "I'm going to bow out." (Then physically retreat from the scene by stepping out or simply walking away.)
- "I'm positive that I can't be helpful here."

- "I wish I had something worthwhile to contribute here, but I don't."

These kinds of statements enable you to withdraw from an argument probably as gracefully as can be done.

Don't tread on my spouse

Suppose you encounter a situation where one or both of your in-laws dump on your spouse. Perhaps they tell you anecdotes about what your spouse did when he or she was younger.

Perhaps they reveal some "deep, dark secrets" they feel you ought to know. If this is within earshot of your spouse and you want to have a long, happy marriage, you probably need to quash this mode of communication as quickly and courteously as possible.

If insights about your spouse are offered outside of his or her earshot, you need to quash this as soon as possible, no matter how juicy or enticing the anecdote is. Why? Turn the tables. Suppose your parents said the same to your spouse when you were not present. How would you feel if you found out later?

Parents and relatives sometimes feel they have the right to dispense such information because, after all, they're talking about their daughter, son, brother, or their sister. They feel that they know this person best and have observations that are long-term and seemingly helpful. Don't fall prey to this maneuver.

You may ask one of your in-laws for help in a particular area in relation to dealing with your spouse, but a major issue arises when they open up the broadcast channel and dispense whatever information they want to about your spouse and you willingly listen.

Here are a variety of potential responses:

- Ask, "Why are you telling me this?" (Wait for their response.) If the response is that your in-law thinks it will help you in your relationship, tell them something along the lines of "I'm already aware of this," "I prefer to find these things out for myself," or "I appreciate your concern but I prefer not to hear this."

- Change the subject. If this works, fine; if it doesn't, change the subject again. If your in-law still won't allow you to do this, try excusing yourself and leaving, using the restroom, or going for a walk.

Here, actions indeed speak louder than words. You send a clear message to your in-laws that this is not the kind of conversation in which you intend to engage. If they don't understand this time, they will the next time you leave.

Are you talking to me?

Suppose your in-laws have a nickname or pet name for you of which you don't approve. Or, suppose they label you in some way behind your back that is less than flattering. In the former case, simply saying, "I prefer to be called Bob" should be sufficient.

If you know your in-laws call you something behind your back or refer to you in some derogatory manner, going out of your way to convince them that you're just the opposite won't work. You'll then mute your own personality and capitulate to their erroneous notions.

As for labels your in-laws may use to refer to you (behind your back or told to you by your spouse), the best advice in terms of standing up for yourself is to ignore it. Such labels might include egghead, dizzy, fashionable, homeboy, and so on.

You need to be yourself with them and away from them. Hopefully, their labels will drop off as they learn more about you, but if they don't, you're better off ignoring the issue. If you challenge or question the image your in-laws have of you, you may never live it down.

Leave me out of this

I wouldn't wish this on you, but suppose one or both of your in-laws are non-stop complainers. Almost every time you encounter them, they yap about the government, economy, media, neighbors, or something else. Suppose they feel the need to place blame on everything large and small for the things that are not going right with the world or their lives.

Misery may or may not like company. The psychic toll that results from complaining and blaming are not worth any fleeting feelings of camaraderie that might surface in your relationship with your in-laws if you decide to join in.

Some people constantly fuel their conversational fires by complaining and blaming. For some, this has become such an ingrained part of their daily routine that they no longer recognize how much of their conversation and thoughts are consumed by negative thoughts. If you start playing their game, hoping to win them over, yours will be a shallow victory.

Social Psychology 101 tells us that if parties A and B have a common enemy C, parties A and B are united. However, that unity lasts only as long as C is present. Suppose that A is your in-laws, B is you, and C is every little thing they complain about or someone in particular.

Remove C, and A and B may find themselves at war with each other. Otherwise, they need D to come along, so they can renew their common dislike of a single target. This approach to forming a relationship does not create much of a union.

Realistically, you're not going to change your in-laws. It took them 60 years to become who they are, and they're perfect at it. They're not going to change in 60 minutes, 60 hours, or 60 days, even if you have a Ph.D. in psychology.

You can politely decline to participate in their complaining and blaming routine by pointing out something to the contrary, as you'll see in the following examples:

- They say, "The government is always trying to squeeze every nickel out of us." You say, "It seems that way sometimes; but the government has sponsored some good programs such as the XYZ."

- They say, "TV is worse than a vast wasteland; it's a sludge pile of porn, violence, and inane sitcoms." You say, "Much of TV is; but, with all the channels we receive today, there are some good programs too. Do you ever watch The Learning Channel, The Discovery Channel, or the Public Education Network?"

- They say, "I don't think that doctors have any clue about what I'm experiencing. With all the money they're making you'd think they'd have some answers." You say, "It's hard for anyone, no matter how educated, experienced, or equipped, to fully understand somebody else's health problem.

By now, you set the drift; no matter what their lament is, you can offer another way to look at the situation. The larger issue is, why bother offering them a counterpoint? Your argument may help, but then again, it may not.

If you offer a counterpoint, it might start an argument. If you don't offer a counterpoint, then politely try to hang in there or change the subject. The choice is yours. At no time, however, should you become a party to their gripe-and-blame game.

Could you say that another way?

Suppose one of your in-laws is notorious for his or her use of profanity. Every other word or sentence offends you. You're not sure if they use profanity for shock effect or if they simply talk this way to everyone. The point is; you don't like it.

It's hard to think of something to say to lessen this person's use of profanity. No matter what you say, you'll sound like a prude to them. One possible strategy, and this is certainly not for everyone, is to let the other party know you're also fully capable of using such language, although you normally choose not to.

If you're not comfortable with the idea of letting out a string of four-letter words, chances are you're not comfortable with this approach. Try excusing yourself from any conversation where you're subjected to language you prefer not to hear. You can always go to the bathroom, the front porch, the backyard, the car, or take a walk around the block.

Previously, you learned that rewarded behavior tends to be repeated. Likewise, you can help extinguish another person's behavior by saying something like, "That kind of language makes me uncomfortable." Or you can withdraw.

If mother-in-law X swears profusely in your presence and so you disappear, mother-in-law X may realize that to continue talking to you, she needs to clean up her act. She may not get your message, though. Either way, you won't be subjected to such language.

Getting family or close friend to listen and respond

With anyone else with whom you are close with, you want to avoid old, unproductive communication patterns, listen carefully to what's being said, and use self-confident language when you want to speak or stand up for yourself.

Remember, the longer you are with someone, the more easily you fall into communication routines. Therefore, it becomes more important to vary the structure of your sentences as well as the substance of your communication. Disarm your listeners on occasion by using bright, bold, colorful language that moves otherwise routine discussions to a new level.

For variety if nothing else, change your sentence patterns constantly. Instead of saying to someone, "I think I can help you here," try, "I see myself striding side-by-side with you as we take control of the situation and devise a system to make things stay in place."

Also, instead of saying, "I've heard what you said, and I'll get back to you," try something like, "What you've said is provocative and certainly merits considerable thought. I'm going to give your words serious attention and offer my plan as to where we can go from here. I appreciate how you've gotten the ball rolling and promise you won't be pushing it alone."

Too exuberant, you say? Disarming? Your communication partner will hardly believe it's you? Fine. That means that your words are likely to be all that more effective!

So...

- The trouble you have with your spouse's parents may have nothing to do with you and everything to do with them. Conversely, check your own behavior and attitudes toward them. Maybe you're the source of the problem.

- You don't have to silently endure behavior from your spouse's parents that you wouldn't tolerate from others.

- All of your relatives deserve respect and understanding. In turn, so do you.

- Sometimes the best way to get your message across is simply to withdraw from a situation and leave the room.

- It's a big and often lonely world, and your relatives can help make it a more hospitable place.

7. Workplace

Now we come to that arena in which being assertive can make the difference between a career that continues to progress at a healthy pace and one that is stifled.

Being self-confident in the workplace, that modern-day jungle is a prerequisite to higher pay, respect, and the corner office. If you doubt it, think about the people with whom you work who are not self-confident. Chances are they're the wimps. They do a good job, perhaps earn a decent wage, but they get passed over time and time again.

In terms of practicing self-esteem skills, the workplace is a special arena. Never mind all that stuff you've seen on inane television shows and movies where executives spar with each other in grandiose ways. There's enough real-life drama that you don't have to draw upon the false images the media conveys.

How, you ask, can self-esteem be a substitute for accomplishment, competence, and effort? Study after study shows that if you and a co-worker have similar education, training, and experience, and all other things about you are equal, the one who is effectively self-confident will predictably rise faster in his or her career.

Suppose two managers are alike in every respect - they have the same background, education, training, aptitude, skills, and so on. You know what this is leading to. One has no problem being professionally self-confident in the following areas:

- Airing his views

- Speaking up for himself

- Defending his turf

- Persuading others

- Speaking up at company meetings

- Making his ideas known

Given that you are a competent employee who fully executes the requirements of the job, the nature of your interpersonal communications at work - how self-confident you are - largely defines your progress.

The other manager is marginally effective in these areas. Who is more likely to rise faster and go further in his career? Okay, you say, this is a no-brainer. Anyone will say the first manager.

Now let's complicate the issue a bit. Suppose that the two managers are alike in most respect, but the first is not quite as sharp, and doesn't quite have some of the technical knowledge possessed by the second manager, but is very good at expressing himself.

The second manager is very conscientious. He is a planner. Generally, he executes his tasks with precision. When it comes to expressing himself, however, there are some gaps in his ability. Sometimes he rambles on. Sometimes he's not forthcoming with his views when the situation calls for it. Sometimes, to know what he's thinking you practically have to pry it out of him. Nevertheless, he does a consistently good job and unquestionably is an asset to the organization.

Now, who's likely to rise faster and further in his career? The answer isn't so easy this time, is it? The odds remain that the first manager will rise faster even if he is lacking in some categories as compared to the second manager. Why? He has the ability to assert himself.

Before you start thinking, okay, well, the first manager has the gift of gab, he's a schmoozer - he talks his way up the chain - think again. The professional who is able to assert himself enjoys significant advantages over his otherwise more talented counterparts who are unassertive. For example, the self-confident professional can do the following:

- Adroitly express himself to others.

- Identify obstacles, hazards, and pitfalls of proceeding with a given plan.

- Better guard against his time when he is already stretched to the max.

- Be more persuasive when influencing others to attain a desirable performance level.

- Establish alliances that can aid him in accomplishing his goals and the goals of others.

What might befall the more technically competent manager who is not as good at asserting himself? The following are all possibilities, although it's not likely that any one manager would be confronted by all of them:

- He ends up taking on more work than he can comfortably handle because he lacks the ability to indicate to others when he's overloaded.

- He may have trouble expressing frustrations over daily occurrences, how a project is going, and so on.

- He may not be as effective in supervising others. He may allow performance levels to slide because he is uneasy when it comes to verbally appraising others' efforts.

Unless we can read each other's minds, the otherwise talented, but unassertive manager, is more likely to be stuck in terms of his overall career progress. He's more likely to stay at the same level longer than his more self-confident counterparts. And, sadly, he's more likely to be overlooked for raises and promotions.

If you doubt that any of this is true and you work in a large office with lots of other career professionals, make a few observations. On a scale of one to ten (with "one" being highly unassertive, and "ten" being highly self-confident) quickly and mentally rate who's in the larger corner office within your organization.

If there's only one corner office, who has it? If there are two, three, or four, who's occupying them? Chances are you'll find self-confident types occupying this prime real estate.

To be sure, there are absolutely brilliant, talented, highly accomplished, non-self-confident career professionals. Someone like that may be seated in your chair right now.

However, if you're not able to convey a sense of importance and even enthusiasm about your accomplishments - not able to "toot your own horn," even though what you've done may be a matter of record - hardly anyone will notice what you've done.

Not even your own boss is likely to grasp the magnitude of your achievement. How could this be? You were asked to do xyz and you did xyz. Doesn't the performance speak for itself? Many times it does. Just as often, probably, the performance does not speak for itself. Perhaps:

- Others take it for granted.

- Others discount in their minds what you've done.

- Others don't recognize the true significance of your deed.

Let's face it, sometimes you may not even understand the value of what you've accomplished, and if that's combined with an inability to assert yourself, you might as well be working in the basement of the building.

The dedicated, hardworking professional in the typical office who consistently does the job day in and day out, but otherwise is unassertive, unfortunately gets passed over when it comes to the goodies and the kudos of work and of life. Here's an exercise to show you how this happens.

Draw up a list of the people in your office. Now go back to the list and put a star next to everyone who got a promotion or someone was rewarded for their good work. For example:

Bill Williamson

Ahmad Maresh

Courtney Adams

Chris Colie

Roxanne Havers

Art Conners

Angela Freeman

Zack Debagan

Katharine Ayers

After you've finished placing stars by the appropriate individuals' names, review the list again. This time put an "A" at the end of the names of all individuals who on a purely personal and subjective scale you deem as being self-confident:

Bill Williamson A

Ahmad Maresh A

Courtnev Adams

Chris Colie A

Roxanne Havers

Angela Freeman

Art Conners

Zack Debagan

Katharine Avers

When you're through, look back at your list. What do you notice? Do most of the people with a star at the beginning of their name have an "A" at the end of their name? Is there a person with simply a star or simply an A and not both? If there is, I'll bet the number is small.

The conclusion? Raises and self-esteem appear to have some significant correlation.

Getting pay raises

Given that you're doing a good job, being self-confident is probably the most important attribute you can have for getting pay raises.

What most people asking for a raise don't understand is that the cost of replacing them can be inordinate. Depending on what you do and how well you do it, your organization may well prefer paying you 5,10, or 15 percent more than you're currently making then having to place an ad, interview more people, bring somebody on board, get them up to speed, and see if they can actually do the job. The smaller the company, the more costly it becomes to replace good staff.

By now, you're probably drooling with anticipation. What exactly do you have to do to get a raise? What are the words? What are the gestures? How does the whole thing work? Actually, it's not complicated at all.

1. Determine in advance how much you want. This has to be in line with other factors, such as the pay range for your position and the budget allocated to your department. If you don't know these things, try to determine what a reasonable percentage increase would be. For example, have others in your firm received 8 percent raises? Or is 4 percent a more predictable figure?

2. Ask your boss for an appointment, or if that's too formal for your setting, at least reserve some time.

Perhaps you can take him or her to lunch. In any case, you want it to be known in advance that you have something important to discuss. Don't go into details about why you want to meet - telling your boss you want to meet to discuss a raise would give him time to prepare his response.

3. Once you're face to face and ready to talk, make sure that both of you are seated. If you're standing, it's too easy for the conversation to be curtailed. The boss might be called away, or you may feel uncomfortable standing your ground for so long. Besides, you'll get more time with the boss if you're seated.

4. Cut right to the chase. By now, your boss knows there's something important on your mind. Let it out.

5. Use the classic irrefutable arguments: You've been doing very good work, you're requiring less supervision, you're anticipating challenges to be better prepared for them, you're helping others on the team, you're going the extra mile, and you're becoming more valuable to the organization, and so on.

If it helps, bring up the parity issues. Other people with your experience, your education, or your age in similar positions in other organizations are earning x amount, and so forth.

Your boss may pooh-pooh your arguments in person; nevertheless, your points will register. If you can, come equipped with specific facts - preferably on paper - to back up these assertions. Instead of just saying you require less supervision, show evidence of a project that you handled alone.

6. If you can get approval at this one meeting, wow, you're a winner! It's more likely that your boss will ask for a follow-up meeting. Agree to it.

7. In the interim, continue to work hard, but don't bring up this issue.

8. When it's time to meet again on this issue, have some new points ready to add on top of the old ones. For example, just last week you were able to accomplish xyz. Also, you took it upon yourself to straighten up the abc project, and you made a few extra calls to make sure of that. Emphasize all the little things you do that nobody tends to notice in addition to those things you do that are more apparent and visible.

9. If you encounter additional resistance, move to, "Okay then, by when?" Get your boss to commit. If she says "next quarter," "by next June," or by next anything, you've done well. Remember, in some

cases, your boss truly is restricted as to what she can offer. Her budget may be fixed for the coming period.

However, there is always some financial slack in an organization when it comes to rewarding and retaining superior performance. You only have to find out what the CEO of your organization is making, including bonuses, and it will be abundantly clear that your organization can find the extra couple dollars per hour or thousands per year you're seeking.

10. Everything you've learned throughout this book about being self-confident comes into play when seeking for a raise. You need to be a good listener. You need to give the other person a chance to respond. You need to look at him directly in the eye. You want to be professionally self-confident but not overbearing or cantankerous. You want to end the conversation on a cheerful note and march proudly back out the door.

Overstating your case is an indication to others that you're grappling with some other issue internally.

If someone is constantly complaining, say about the weather, the reality is he probably isn't really concerned with the weather as something else.

When you assert yourself, make sure that the time, place, and person are appropriate. It doesn't matter how self-confident you are if you ask someone to do something that he:

1. Can't understand in 100 years of explanation

2. Have no capacity or authority for undertaking

3. Might be able to accomplish but doesn't know where to begin

Offer your points in sequence based on chronology, order of importance, or other useful criterion. Some communication experts tell you to present your best point first, and your other points in descending order of importance.

Other communication experts suggest that you present your points in ascending order; that is, start with the least important ones and work up to the most important one. In this manner, the last point that you make is your best and most important and the one most likely to be remembered by your audience.

In my opinion it doesn't matter in what order you proceed - ascending, descending, or even offering your best point in the middle. More importantly is that you did a good job to begin with; you prepped your boss so that he or she knew that you were coming in to talk about something important. You reviewed the tips throughout this book, and you were most confident when you finally sat down and started the conversation about your value to the organization.

8. Miscellaneous Tips

Too many people erroneously believe they have to be some type of exalted being to be self-confident because, after all, self-confident people never blow their tops. Au contraire! Anybody can get angry, even the most highly self-confident people.

However, the assertive, self-confident person expresses his anger in a constructive manner as opposed to a destructive way (such as by shouting, threatening, insulting, or otherwise abusing others).

A paragon is a model of perfection or excellence - having no equal. Hence, no one is a paragon of self-confidence or self-esteem.

Likewise, the assertive, self-confident person handles other challenges in a similar manner. More specifically, they:

- Identify what's needed

- Express how they feel

- Indicate what needs to be done

- Refer to the bigger picture

- Elicit agreement or cooperation

- Close the discussion cordially

There are people, and you may know some, who are self-confident most of the time. Sure, they face challenges ahead of them, and like anybody, they can "lose it" on occasion. Generally, though, they approach each day and most situations with relative grace and ease. You can almost feel the calmness disseminating from the center of their being.

Paradoxically, self-confident people don't strive to be self-confident. It's almost as if they just allow themselves to "be." They seem to tap into internal resources that perhaps have been there all along.

Self-confident people let vital qualities rise to the surface. They're not at war with themselves. Think of it - how would it feel if you were so self-assured that no one could shake your view of yourself?

Certainly, self-confident people have doubts about themselves, their work, and their lives in general. However, rather than try to force themselves to think and see everything as positive, they allow their doubts to be part of the total mix of their experiences.

They don't allow their doubts to rule them. They maintain a level of honesty within themselves. They think, feel, sort, and automatically redirects them toward the most appropriate thinking, behavior, and action.

A successful high school basketball coach was once asked by one of his mentors to join the college ranks as an assistant coach. This would mean an increase in salary and, perhaps, a chance to work as a head coach in college someday. The high school coach thought about it and said, "I'm flattered, but I have to decline. I know what I am; I'm a high school coach."

Did he show a lack of ambition, or was he simply being true to himself?

Optimism doesn't necessarily equate with high self-confidence. You can be pessimistic but self-confident. But if you are naturally optimistic, your ability to develop or maintain self-confidence is probably enhanced.

Conclusion

There are people in my life, and undoubtedly in yours, who, when they say something, prompted you to act. It's something in the way they speak - their measured tones, often speaking in a deeper bass voice that summons something within us to take notice.

If you have never regarded your voice as a tool for being more self-confident in this life, you're in for some revelations. I'm not going to ask you to change your voice. (Unless you have already repeatedly received feedback to the contrary, chances are, you don't need to make it lower or higher.)

By practicing what you learn in this book, you'll make the best of the voice God gave you. As with all change, you can't expect a miracle overnight. It's about setting some reasonable expectations for yourself.
Everything presented here may not be your cup of tea, but by following what is recommended in this book one step at a time, you'll rack up small achievements that will spur you on to even greater confidence.

May I ask a small favor from you? If you can find the time, can you please leave an honest review for this book? Whether it is good or bad, I would really appreciate it! I am always striving to improve my book. Thank You!